Simply Bar[oque]

27 Well Known Masterpieces

Arranged by Bruce Nelson

Simply Baroque is a collection of arias, choral works, concerto themes, dances, and keyboard and string masterpieces from the Baroque period of music history (ca. 1600–1750). These selections have been carefully arranged by Bruce Nelson for Easy Piano, making them accessible to pianists of all ages. Phrase markings, fingering, pedaling and dynamics have been included to aid with interpretation, and a large print size makes the notation easy to read.

The Baroque period has a diverse and exciting body of music. Some of the world's most beloved melodies come from this era. Johann Pachelbel's "Canon in D" and Johann Sebastian Bach's "Jesu, Joy of Man's Desiring" have become favorite selections for wedding services. Handel's "Hallelujah Chorus" is one of the most uplifting pieces of music heard around the holiday season. Baroque music can be lyrical and poignant as in Henry Purcell's "When I Am Laid in Earth," an aria from his opera *Dido and Aenaes*. It can also be energetic and jubilant as in Antonio Vivaldi's "Gloria," a sacred work rediscovered in the 1930s, which has become greatly popular with church choirs. With its ability to capture the spirit of dance, the wonder of the divine, and the joy of life, this music has been embraced by musicians and audiences, young and old, around the world. For these reasons and more, the Baroque selections on the following pages are exciting to explore.

After all, this is *Simply Baroque!*

ISBN-10: 0-7390-5181-4
ISBN-13: 978-0-7390-5181-8

Alfred

Contents

Arrival of the Queen of Sheba

(from *Solomon*)

George Frideric Handel
Arranged by Bruce Nelson

Brandenburg Concerto No. 3
(Allegro)

Johann Sebastian Bach
Arranged by Bruce Nelson

rit.

Canon in D

Johann Pachelbel
Arranged by Bruce Nelson

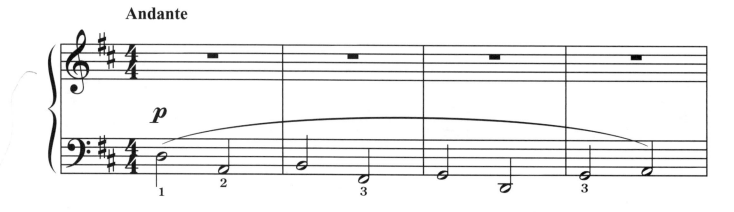

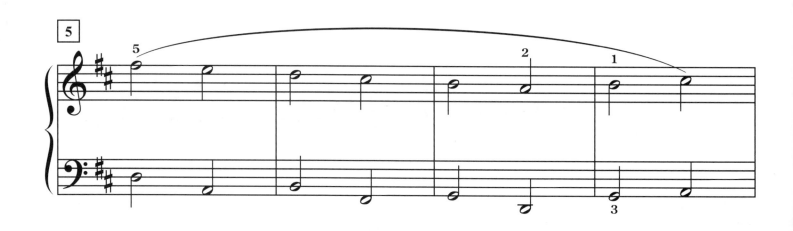

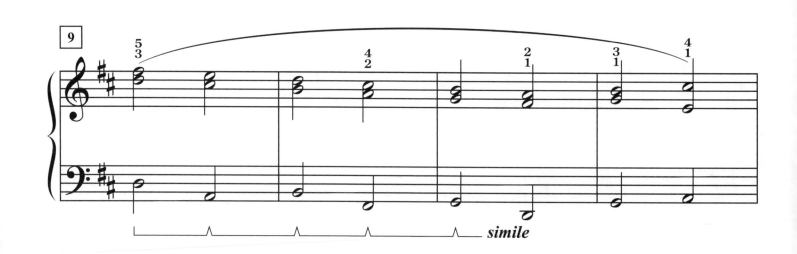

Cello Suite No. 1 in G Major
(Prelude)

Johann Sebastian Bach
Arranged by Bruce Nelson

Christmas Concerto
(Adagio)

Arcangelo Corelli
Arranged by Bruce Nelson

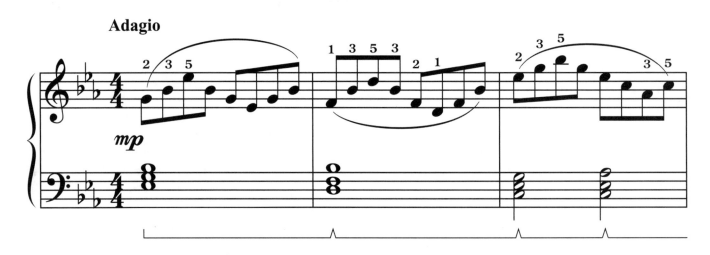

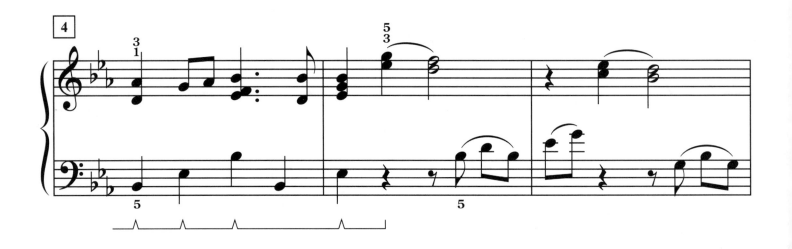

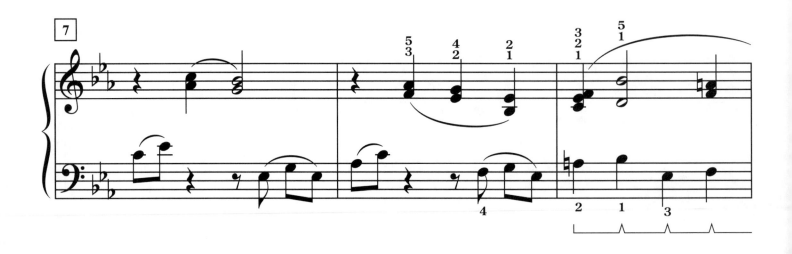

Christmas Concerto
(Allegro)

Arcangelo Corelli
Arranged by Bruce Nelson

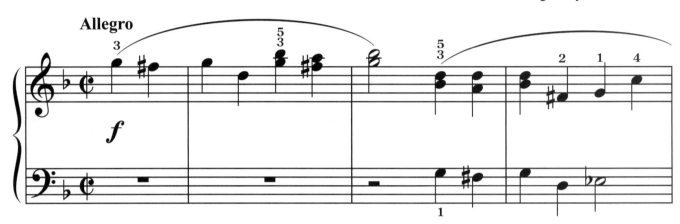

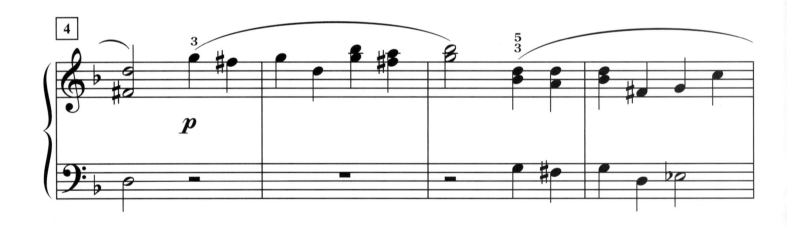

Concerto a due cori No. 2

(Allegro ma non troppo)

George Frideric Handel
Arranged by Bruce Nelson

Allegro ma non troppo

LH detached

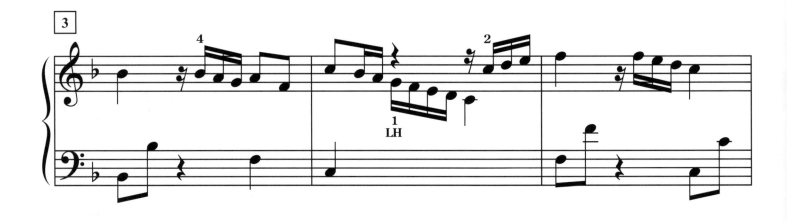

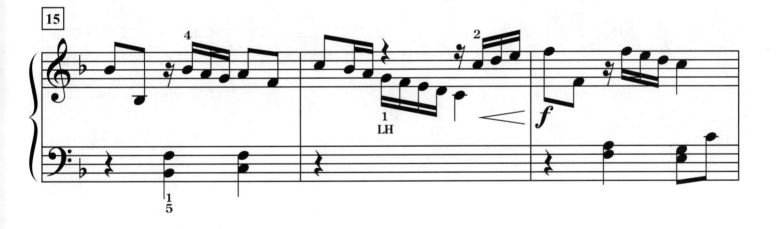

Concerto in D Major
(Largo)

Antonio Vivaldi
Arranged by Bruce Nelson

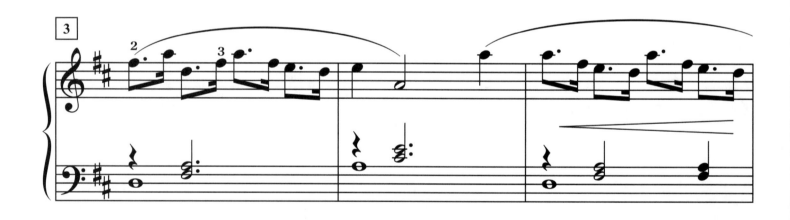

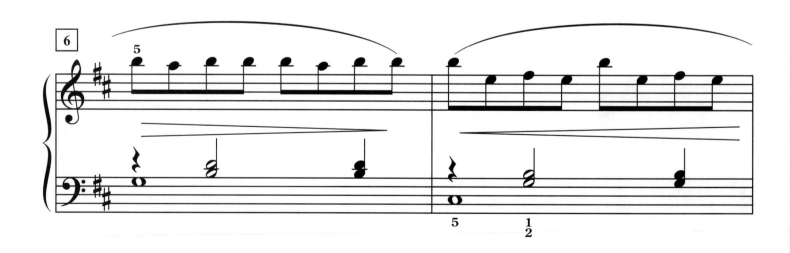

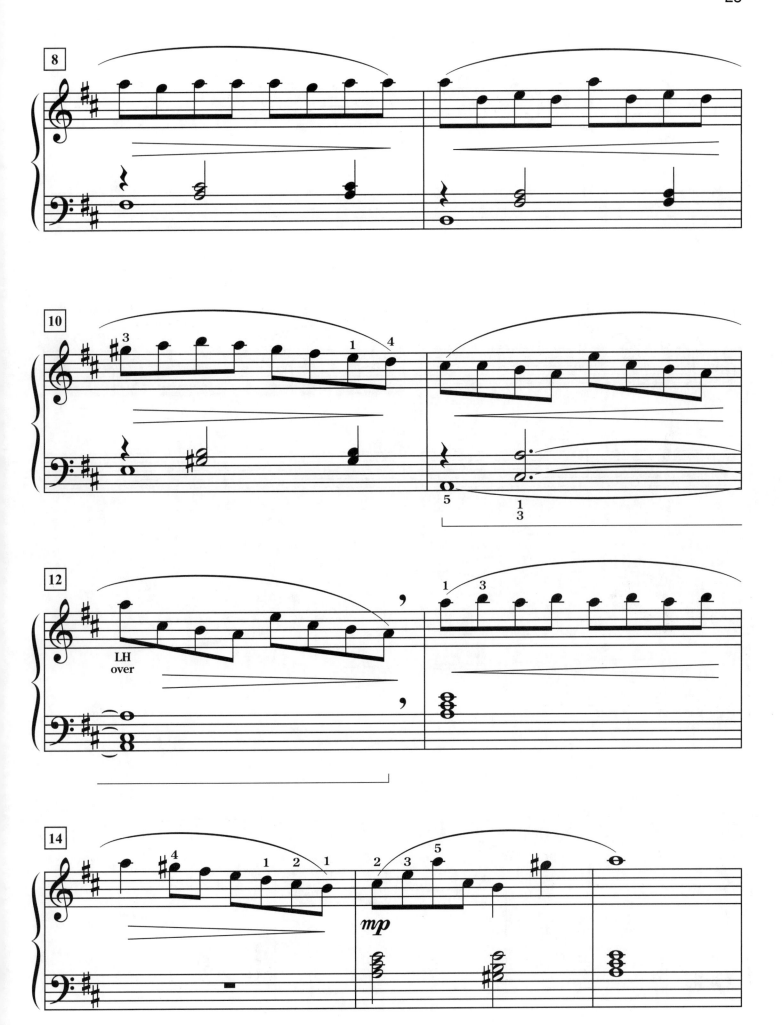

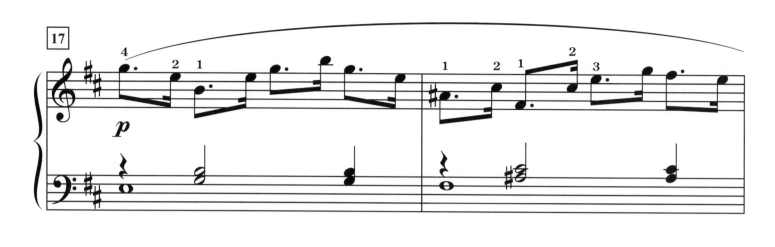

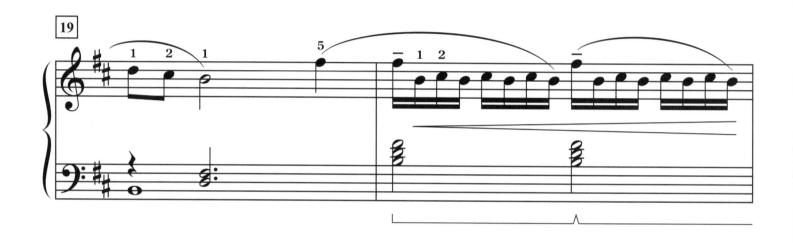

Gloria

Antonio Vivaldi
Arranged by Bruce Nelson

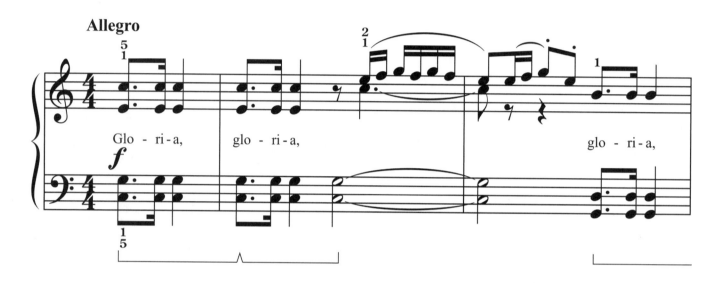

Hallelujah Chorus
(from *Messiah*)

George Frideric Handel
Arranged by Bruce Nelson

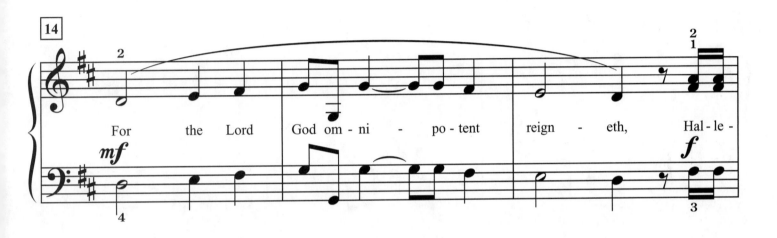

Hornpipe
(from *Water Music*)

George Frideric Handel
Arranged by Bruce Nelson

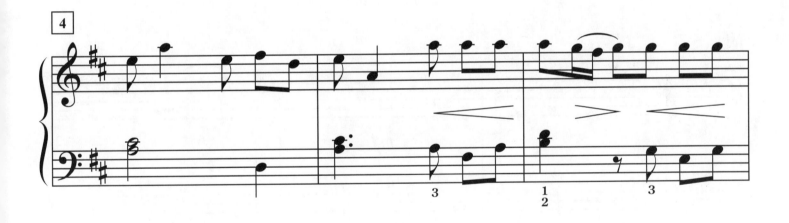

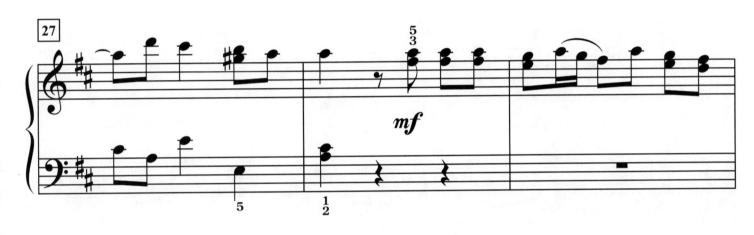

Jesu, Joy of Man's Desiring

Johann Sebastian Bach
Arranged by Bruce Nelson

Mandolin Concerto in C Major

(Allegro)

Antonio Vivaldi
Arranged by Bruce Nelson

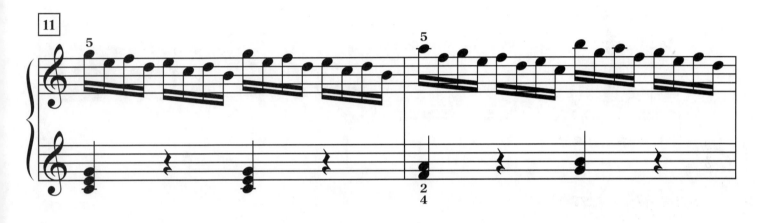

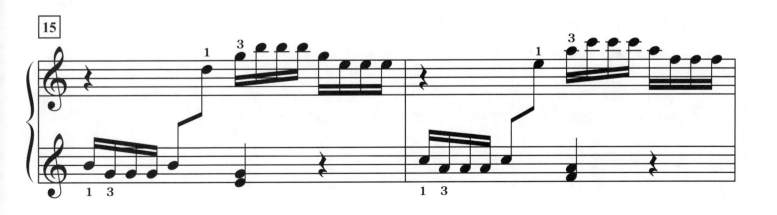

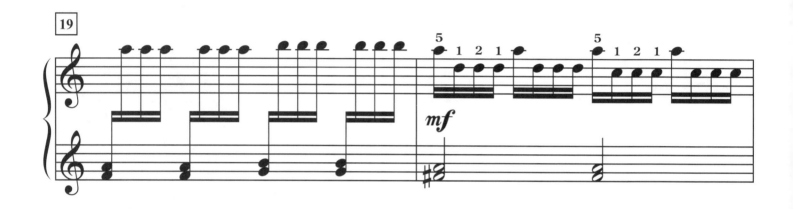

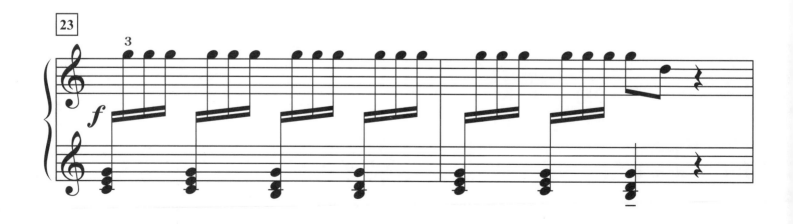

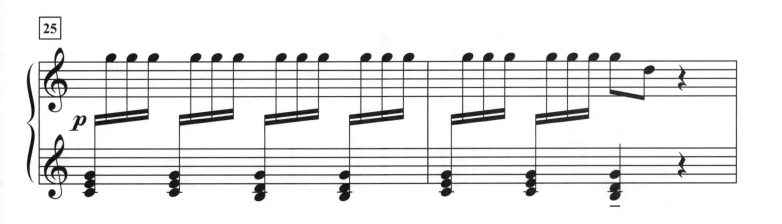

poco a poco cresc.

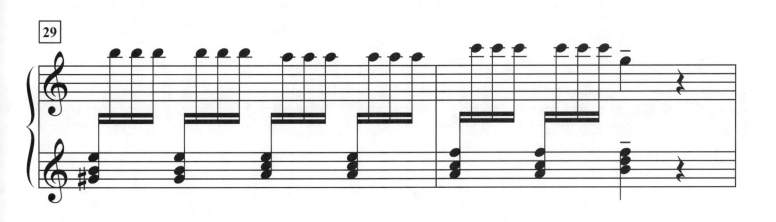

Minuet in G Major

(from J.S. Bach's *Notebook for Anna Magdalena Bach*)

Christian Petzold

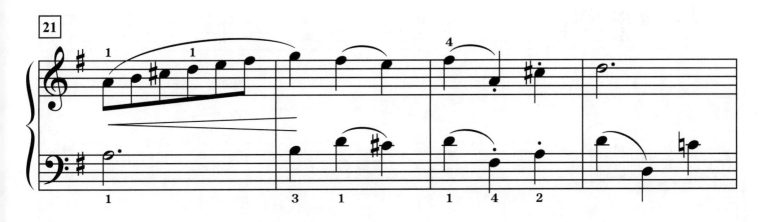

Prelude

(from *Te Deum*)

Marc-Antoine Charpentier
Arranged by Bruce Nelson

Prince of Denmark's March

Jeremiah Clarke
Arranged by Bruce Nelson

Ombra mai fù

(from *Serse*)

George Frideric Handel
Arranged by Bruce Nelson

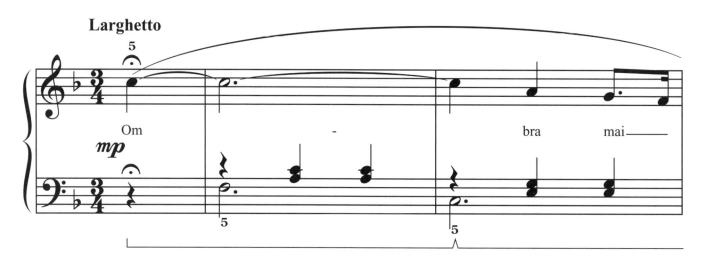

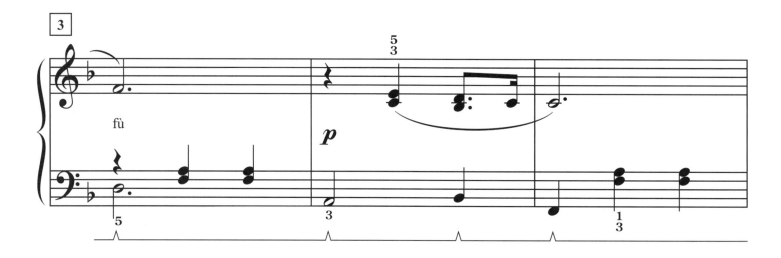

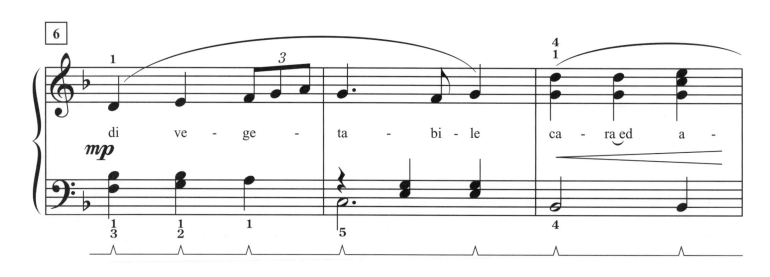

Rondeau
(from *Suite de symphonies*)

Jean-Joseph Mouret
Arranged by Bruce Nelson

Allegro maestoso

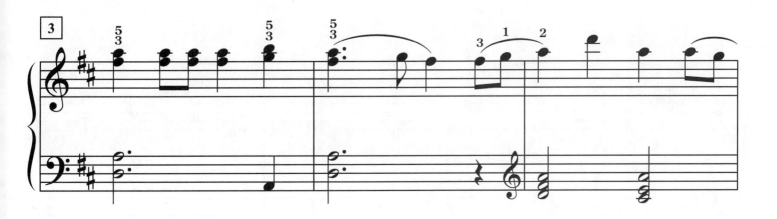

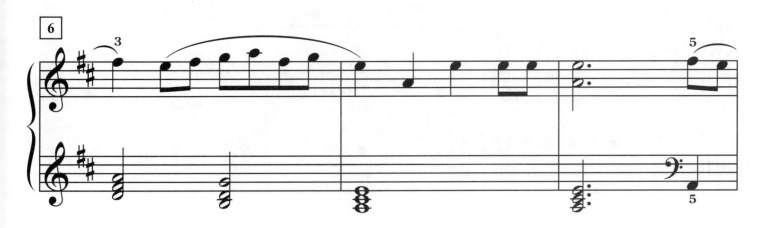

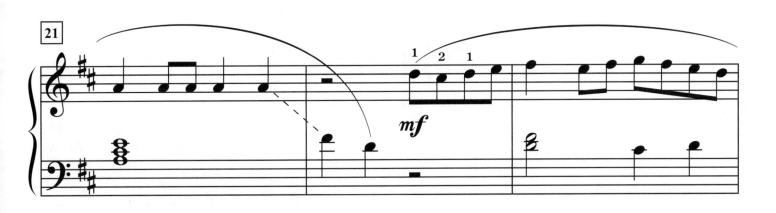

Rondeau

(from *Abdelazer*)

Henry Purcell
Arranged by Bruce Nelson

Allegro maestoso

Sonata in G Major

Domenico Scarlatti
Arranged by Bruce Nelson

Allegro

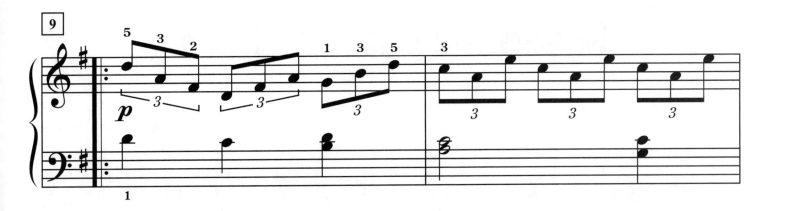

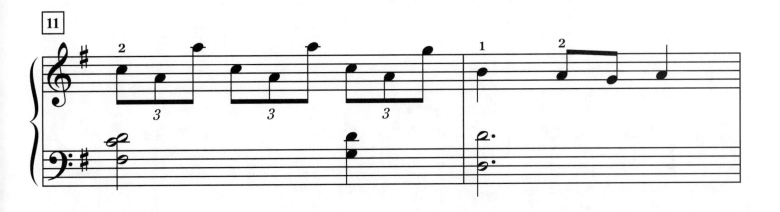

Sheep May Safely Graze

Johann Sebastian Bach
Arranged by Bruce Nelson

Spring

(from *The Four Seasons*)

Antonio Vivaldi
Arranged by Bruce Nelson

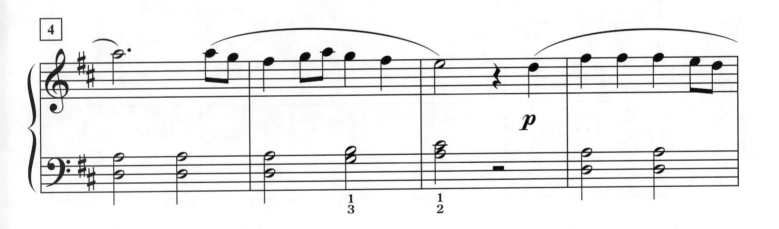

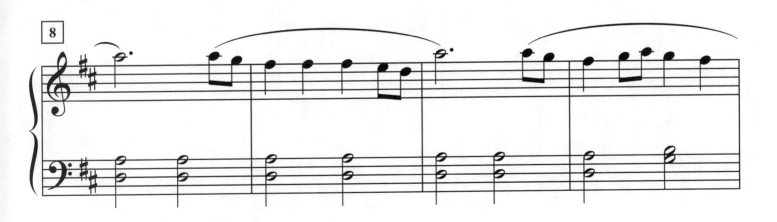

Tambourin
(Drum Song)

Jean-Philippe Rameau
Arranged by Bruce Nelson

Allegretto

Toccata

(from *L'Orfeo*)

Claudio Monteverdi
Arranged by Bruce Nelson

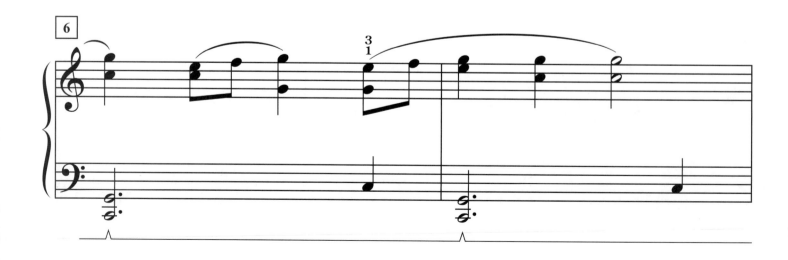

Toccata in D Minor

Johann Sebastian Bach
Arranged by Bruce Nelson

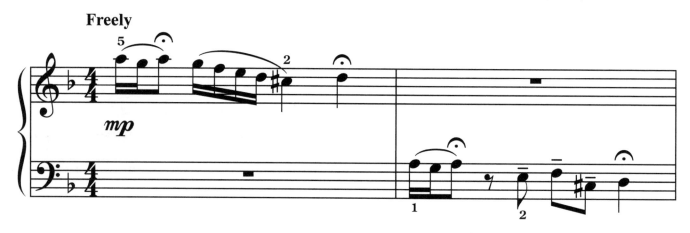

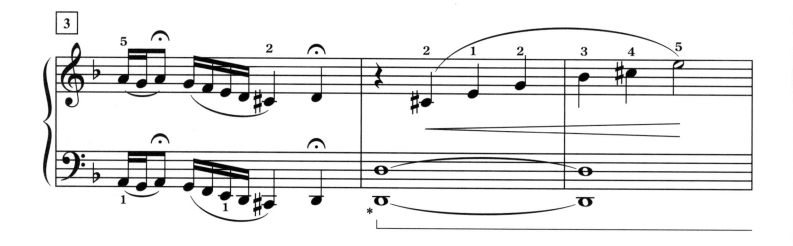

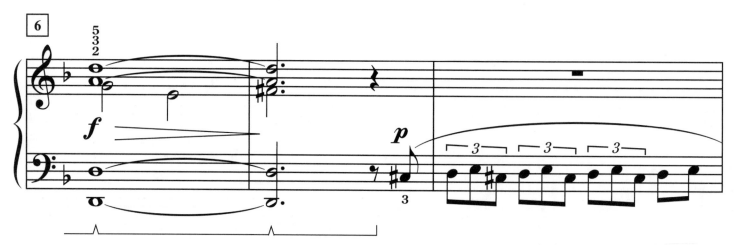

* The octaves in measures 4–7 may be played one octave lower.

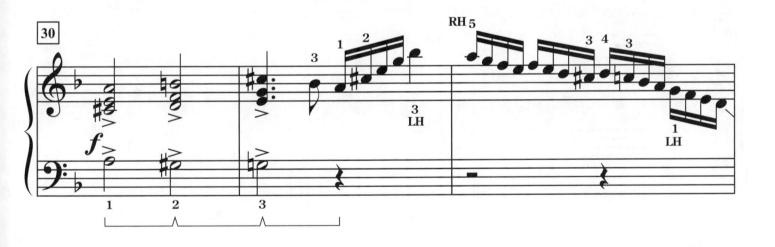

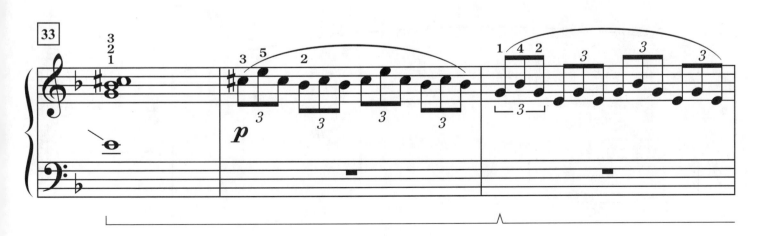

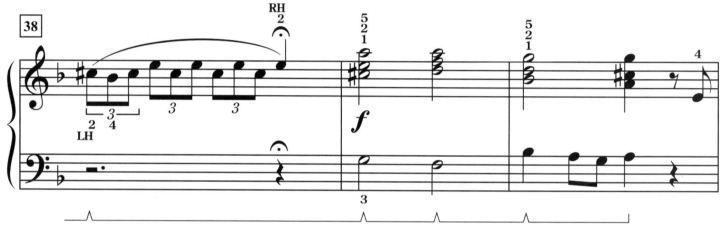

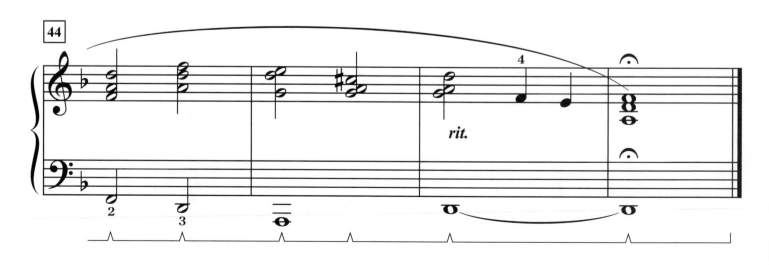

Viola Concerto in G Major

(Largo)

Georg Philipp Telemann
Arranged by Bruce Nelson

When I Am Laid in Earth

(from *Dido and Aenaes*)

Henry Purcell
Arranged by Bruce Nelson